Data collection

Student text and unit guide

The School Mathematics Project

CAMBRIDGE
UNIVERSITY PRESS

Main authors	Chris Belsom
	Richard Coe
	Stan Dolan
	Jane Southern
	Roger Stern

| Team Leader | Chris Belsom |

| Project director | Stan Dolan |

Initial work on this unit was carried out by members of the Department of Applied Statistics at the University of Reading. Several others have helped with advice and criticism.

The authors would like to give special thanks to Ann White for her help in preparing this book for publication.

Cartoons by Paul Holland

Photographs by Ken Cockram

Published by the Press Syndicate of the University of Cambridge
The Pitt Building, Trumpington Street, Cambridge CB2 1RP
40 West 20th Street, New York, NY 10011-4211, USA
10 Stamford Road, Oakleigh, Victoria 3166, Australia

First published 1992

Produced by 16-19 Mathematics, Southampton

Printed in Great Britain by Scotprint Ltd., Musselburgh.

ISBN 0 521 42646 4

Contents and resources

Items in *italics* refer to resources not included in this text.

Introduction to the unit

Statistics, as taught in schools and higher education, often starts with data, with little attention paid to where the data come from. This unit is about **collecting** data – how this should be planned and carried out. The principles of designing studies of data collection are developed with reference to two broad types of sampling procedures, surveys and experiments.

Students should have met some of the concepts covered in *Living with uncertainty* before this unit is attempted. Otherwise, the unit is independent of other *16-19 Mathematics* texts.

This unit has been written to facilitate 'supported self study':

- All solutions and commentaries are in this text.

- A special tutorial sheet can be used to focus discussion at a final tutorial on the work of each chapter.

By having the student text and unit guide combined and by not having lengthy exercises the text of *Data collection* has been designed to put the emphasis on each student's own practical work. The planning of a data collection requires practical understanding and students will improve their knowledge of the principles of design by trying to apply the ideas introduced in this unit to their own surveys and experiments.

Chapter 1

The opening chapter introduces the two ways in which data may be collected, by survey or by experiment. A number of examples are used to illustrate the need for careful 'design' in the setting-up of a sampling procedure.

Chapter 2

The main sampling methods in this chapter are random sampling, stratified sampling and quota sampling. The work is centred upon a simple survey to estimate the number of trees in a forest. The data collection is carried out in two different ways and the important issue is which method is better and why.

The idea of the forest sample is based upon practical work developed at the Department of Applied Statistics, University of Reading. The original form of this practical uses a large piece of thick card, with a river painted down the middle. Onto this are stuck small, numbered pieces of card. They are hinged so that the data for that area can be read if that card is sampled. You might like to bring this practical to life by making your own version of this equipment.

Chapter 3

This chapter introduces some of the ways in which statistics are used in food studies. Three designs for taste tests are described, the triangle test, the duo-trio test and the pairs difference test. An important common theme is the need to avoid bias by using a balanced design, so that all possible sequences of the products being sampled occur equally often in the experiment.

Chapter 4

This chapter opens by considering the statistical, practical and ethical issues involved in the testing of drugs. Various designs for experiments are then introduced and compared. Parallel groups, matched-pair, crossover and permuted block designs are all considered.

Chapter 5

The first four chapters of this unit introduce a number of important statistical ideas in an intuitive and practical way. This final chapter summarises some of the ideas and gives an overview of a few of the underlying principles of sampling, such as the concepts of replication and randomisation.

1 Data and inference

1.1 Data, data everywhere!

The collection, analysis and interpretation of information have a very high public profile. The following three examples of statistical articles are taken from a national newspaper on a single day.

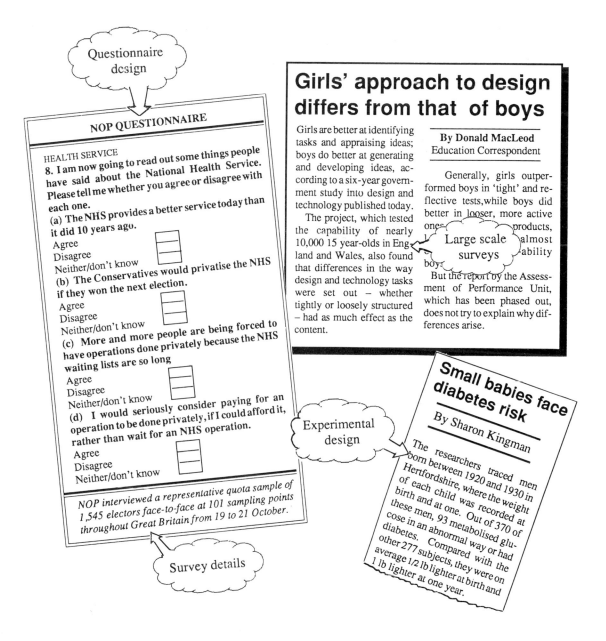

Questionnaire design

NOP QUESTIONNAIRE

HEALTH SERVICE

8. I am now going to read out some things people have said about the National Health Service. Please tell me whether you agree or disagree with each one.

(a) The NHS provides a better service today than it did 10 years ago.

Agree
Disagree
Neither/don't know

(b) The Conservatives would privatise the NHS if they won the next election.

Agree
Disagree
Neither/don't know

(c) More and more people are being forced to have operations done privately because the NHS waiting lists are so long

Agree
Disagree
Neither/don't know

(d) I would seriously consider paying for an operation to be done privately, if I could afford it, rather than wait for an NHS operation.

Agree
Disagree
Neither/don't know

NOP interviewed a representative quota sample of 1,545 electors face-to-face at 101 sampling points throughout Great Britain from 19 to 21 October.

Survey details

Girls' approach to design differs from that of boys

Girls are better at identifying tasks and appraising ideas; boys do better at generating and developing ideas, according to a six-year government study into design and technology published today.

The project, which tested the capability of nearly 10,000 15 year-olds in England and Wales, also found that differences in the way design and technology tasks were set out – whether tightly or loosely structured – had as much effect as the content.

By Donald MacLeod
Education Correspondent

Generally, girls outperformed boys in 'tight' and reflective tests, while boys did better in looser, more active ones products, almost ability boys

Large scale surveys

But the report by the Assessment of Performance Unit, which has been phased out, does not try to explain why differences arise.

Experimental design

Small babies face diabetes risk

By Sharon Kingman

The researchers traced men born between 1920 and 1930 in Hertfordshire, where the weight of each child was recorded at birth and at one. Out of 370 of these men, 93 metabolised glucose in an abnormal way or had diabetes. Compared with the other 277 subjects, they were on average 1/2 lb lighter at birth and 1 lb lighter at one year.

The Independent, 25 October 1991

You need to be careful about **how** you collect information. For example, a potentially embarrassing question may not produce an honest response. A national newspaper, in an attempt to find out if people actually read the books they buy, proceeded as outlined in the article below.

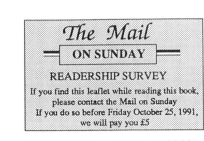

The Mail
ON SUNDAY

READERSHIP SURVEY

If you find this leaflet while reading this book, please contact the Mail on Sunday. If you do so before Friday October 25, 1991, we will pay you £5

SURVEY: The printed note hidden inside 240 novels

Four weeks ago, when the Booker jury announced the short-list of six novels, we visited book shops in London, Brighton, Oxford, Cambridge, Stratford-upon-Avon and Bath.

We secretly slid a small printed and numbered note into 40 copies of each of the six nominated novels – 240 in all.

The notes were placed two-thirds of the way through each book, jammed hard against the spine so they could not be shaken out, yet were impossible to miss by anyone who actually opened that particular page.

Five pounds was offered to finders who telephoned a special number before last Friday.

We know all the books were sold. We checked this week with the bookshops and the publishers. At each of our survey bookshops the short-listed novels were re-ordered and the publishers had reprinted runs ranging from 6,000 to 15,000 copies.

Response

Yet, come the deadline, we had received only 19 calls – less than eight per cent of the total.

When NOP inserts questionnaires into magazines, with almost no incentive to readers to fill in the answers and post them off, the response rate is 20 to 30 per cent.

And the survey sample was not too small to draw conclusions. After all, elections have been timed on national surveys of only 1,000 people.

The Mail on Sunday, 27 October 1991

> **Comment on the 'design' of this survey.**

This unit aims to help you think about the **collection** of data – deciding exactly **what** data you need and **how** to go about collecting it. Statistical data are subject to considerable abuse and no amount of clever analysis can make up for inadequate data collection.

1.2 Survey and experiment

There are two ways in which data may be collected in response to a particular problem, by **survey** or by **experiment.**

In a survey, information is gathered under existing conditions in an attempt to determine some particular characteristic(s) of a population.

In an experiment, comparisons are made between two or more groups under strictly controlled conditions where the factor that is being tested is the only variable. A trial to ascertain the effectiveness of a particular drug is a good example of an experiment.

A biology class proposes to investigate the effect of water temperature on the growth rate of tadpoles. They have 150 tadpoles, together with a number of jars with thermostats, and have decided to compare temperatures of 10°C, 15°C and 20°C.

Discuss the design of this investigation and consider general ideas that might be useful in the design of other investigations.

The key differences between surveys and experiments are summarised below.

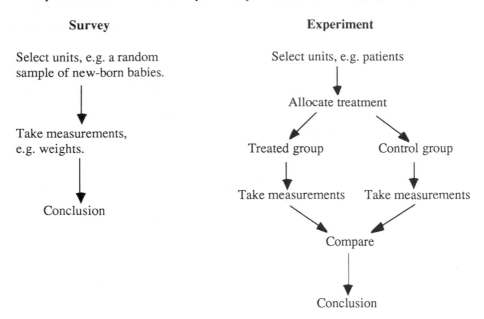

Survey	Experiment

Survey:
Select units, e.g. a random sample of new-born babies.
↓
Take measurements, e.g. weights.
↓
Conclusion

Experiment:
Select units, e.g. patients
↓
Allocate treatment
↙ ↘
Treated group   Control group
↓   ↓
Take measurements   Take measurements
↘   ↙
Compare
↓
Conclusion

In Chapter 2 you will explore some of the features of surveys. Experiments are covered in Chapters 3 and 4.

After working through this chapter you should:

1. be more aware of potential problems when collecting data and, in particular, know that you should always define properly what you want to measure;

2. know that statistical information may be collected either by

    (a) surveys

    or

    (b) experiments

    and be aware of the differences between these methods.

Tutorial sheet

1.

Mixed results for local schools

By Staff Reporter Sally Waghorn

Broadgreen Middle School and Longlane Village School had contrasting results in a national test of reading ages for 11-year-olds.

School	Average reading age
Broadgreen	10.1
Longlane	12.2

(a)   From the extract above, what can be inferred about the performances of the two schools?

(b)   Describe how you might assess the performance of a school.

2.   You are to investigate whether the weight of a new-born baby is likely to be affected if the mother smokes during pregnancy.

Discuss the advantages of doing this by:

(a)   collecting appropriate data from a survey;

(b)   setting up an experiment.

2 *Survey methods*

2.1 Introduction

Conducting a survey is a commonly used method of obtaining information about a population. So that you do not have to count or measure **every** member, it is usual to obtain information from a **sample** of the population.

> **A survey provides information about a population from a sample of the population.**

To ensure that there is no selection bias, each member of the sample is usually chosen by a random process. Even when the sample is selected correctly, other factors are important in ensuring that the data provide representative information about a population.

 A town planning department wishes to use a survey to discover what facilities may be required in a sports centre they intend to build. Describe how they might obtain the information and any problems they may encounter in ensuring that they have the representative views of those living in the town.

2.2   A forest survey

In the process of statistical analysis, too little thought is sometimes given to the actual collection of the data. This is guaranteed to lead to mistaken conclusions and embarrassing errors.

> **It is always important to know *how* data have been collected.**

In this chapter you will consider some of the essential aspects of survey methods by looking at an example of a forest survey.

Forest plantations cover 10% of the total land area of Great Britain – more than 2.1 million hectares. Almost half of this area is owned by the Forestry Commission and the remainder by private owners, ranging from individuals to large estates and companies. The managements of these plantations employ around 30 000 people and require good estimates of the quantity and quality of timber involved.

Suppose a forest plot, consisting of pine trees of the same age, is to be sold.

Suppose further that you need to estimate the number of trees standing on the plot and the proportion which may be classified as large.

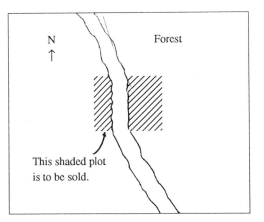

Assuming that there are too many trees to count individually, the plot might be divided into a number of sampling areas. Suppose that there are 72 such areas on the west side of a river and another 96 on the east side. Information is collected from 14 of the areas.

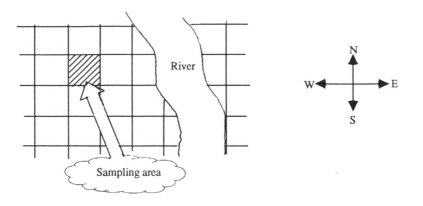

Sampling area

River

N
W ← → E
S

(a)   **What information do you need to collect from each area? What practical problems may need to be overcome when collecting such information?**

(b)   **Will 14 of the areas prove sufficient for the sample?**

TASKSHEET 1 – *To the woods!*

The tasksheet gave results based on two methods of sampling, which can be described as follows:

> A *simple random sample* is one where every member of the population has an equal chance of being selected.
>
> For a population made up of a number of sub-groups, or *strata*, a *stratified sample* is one where each stratum is sampled separately. In the simplest form of stratified sample, the number chosen from each stratum is proportional to the size of that stratum.

2.3   Choosing a stratified sample

If an estimate produced by one sampling scheme is likely to be better than that produced by another, then the first scheme is said to have greater **precision.**

One way to improve the precision of a scheme is simply to increase the size of the sample. However, a larger sample involves greater time and cost and so other methods of improving precision are preferred.

> **A good sampling scheme is one which achieves precision from relatively small samples.**

 TASKSHEET 2 – *Improving precision*

One practical way of improving precision is to use stratified sampling. To be effective, the stratification chosen should split the population into groups whose means are as different as possible.

> **Describe how you might choose the strata in a survey to estimate the amount of money per week spent on entertainment by 16-19 year olds.**

It is not necessary to sample each stratum equally. If one of the strata is very variable and another more uniform, then you should concentrate your efforts on the more variable stratum.

> **Suppose you have to predict the support for the various political parties in a forthcoming general election. Suppose further that the electorate has been divided into strata according to age and profession. Explain why it might be appropriate to sample more heavily from the young and from white collar workers.**

2.4   Questionnaire design

For reasons discussed earlier, stratification of a sample is generally carried out in large surveys. Market researchers are often asked to interview a random sample consisting of a particular number of people of each gender and from several age or social groups. For example, a female lawyer aged 38 may belong to a stratum defined as:

female, professional, age 30-39

An example of a very large survey is the National Food Survey, which was introduced during the Second World War and is still carried out each year. A sample of house-holders are asked to record how much food they buy during one week and how much it costs.

> **How would you stratify for the National Food Survey?**

In large surveys of this type it is impractical to interview participants and so a questionnaire is used instead. Many design features of a 'good' questionnaire are simply common sense.

*   It is crucial to define exactly what it is that you want to measure. You should avoid asking unnecessary questions and gathering information which cannot be used. In addition you do not want the questionnaire to be so long that it puts people off!

*   Each question must be worded so that it is easy to understand and unambiguous. This is especially important if respondents have to fill in the questionnaire themselves.

*   If a question is sensitive, then it has to be asked particularly carefully so as not to give offence. Sensitive questions should be avoided at the beginning of the questionnaire.

*   Each question should be formulated in an unbiased way.

*   It is usually best to start with easy questions. Think of a logical order from one topic to the next. Start each topic with general questions and then go on to more specific ones.

*   Before a questionnaire is used in a large-scale study, it should be tested in a 'pilot study'.

> **Describe some of the design features in the following extract of a questionnaire on milk consumption.**

Milk Questionnaire

We are undertaking some research to find out how we can improve our service to you. Your help in completing this questionnaire would be very much appreciated.

Please read through each question and answer each one by ticking or filling in the box corresponding with your reply.

Q1   How many members of your household are there?

1 ☐   2 ☐   3 ☐   4 ☐   5 or more ☐

Q2   In an average week where do you buy milk?

Doorstep delivery ☐   Supermarket ☐   (Tick one or
Small shop ☐   Farm ☐   more boxes)

Other (please specify) ☐ ....

Q3   In an average week does your household buy semi-skimmed milk?

Yes ☐   No ☐

If you answered yes please answer questions 4 and 5. Otherwise proceed to question 6.

Q4   In an average week how many pints of semi-skimmed milk does your household buy? ☐

Some questions are **closed response** questions. The respondent has to choose one or more answers from a list or give a rating on a scale which is provided.

Other questions are **open response**. Respondents are not restricted in their answers.

> (a)   What would be an open response question format for question 2?
>
> (b)   Suggest some of the advantages and disadvantages of open response questions. What are the advantages and disadvantages of closed response questions?
>
> (c)   Discuss the actual format of question 2 in the light of your answers to (b).

One of the main problems with questionnaires concerns the fact that bias may be introduced because of major differences between those who return a completed questionnaire and those who do not. This problem can be partially offset by selecting from the completed forms a fixed number of forms for various strata that have previously been defined.

An alternative to the use of questionnaires is telephone sampling.

> Describe some of the advantages and disadvantages of telephone sampling.

2.5   Opinion polls

Questions about people's opinions are asked in various forms of survey and there are several organisations which regularly survey public opinion. The Gallup Poll is a monthly survey in which questions are asked about important current issues and politics. Gallup was the first such poll and was founded in 1936. Two similar monthly surveys are the Harris Poll and the National Opinion Poll. The results of the surveys are published in different newspapers.

POLLS SINCE CHRISTMAS					
Poll	Fieldwork	Sample	Con %	Lab %	Lib Dem %
MORI	27 Dec	1,087	38	44	14
NOP	7-8 Jan	1,046	40	45	13
Gallup	8-13 Jan	1,115	42	37.5	16
ICM	10-11 Jan	1,468	42	41	12
NOP	11-13 Jan	1,453	40	43	13

The Independent, 18 January 1992

The Harris Poll and the National Opinion Poll use random sampling. Every member of the public is equally likely to have his or her opinions sought by those conducting these surveys.

The Gallup Poll uses **quota sampling**. Each interviewer is told how many men and women to question, as well as how many from each age group and social class. It is then left to the interviewers to choose the actual individuals they will question. Although stratification is used, the choice of people within each stratum is not necessarily random.

As well as using different types of sampling, different polls use samples of different sizes. They also ask questions in different areas of interest.

When a general election is approaching, the opinion polls attract much attention. However, the data have to be treated cautiously. In 1970, the results of most of the pre-election polls suggested a Labour win, but in the event the Conservatives won.

> **Suggest possible reasons for the incorrect predictions of the polls in 1970.**

After working through this chapter you should:

1.   understand the terms random sample and stratified sample;

2.   know what is meant by the precision of an estimate;

3.   understand some of the advantages of stratified surveys;

4.   be aware of some of the issues connected with the use of questionnaires and telephone polls;

5.   be sufficiently confident to conduct a survey of your own.

To the woods!

You will need Datasheet 1, *Forestry data,* and a means of generating random numbers. The datasheet provides the necessary information on the trees in 168 areas of the forest, each area being a five-hectare rectangle.

The task is to estimate the total number of trees on the plot being sold and the proportion of large trees on the plot.

It is considered that sampling 14 of the areas will be sufficient.

Two different **sampling schemes** are proposed - schemes A and B. You should conduct the survey using each scheme in turn.

Sampling scheme A – Select 14 areas at random from the 168 on the plot.

1.   How can you select 14 numbers from 1 to 168 inclusive? Is your method efficient?

2.   Devise a suitable table for recording your results. Select the areas and record the appropriate data.

3.   Calculate the mean of the 14 values. Hence estimate

    (a)   the numbers of trees on the plot;

    (b)   the number of large trees on the plot;

    (c)   the proportion of large trees on the plot.

Sampling scheme B – Select 6 areas at random from the west of the river (Region 1) and 8 from the east (Region 2).

4.   Why do you think the numbers 6 and 8 have been used?

5.   Devise a suitable means of selecting the areas and a table for recording your results. Results for the two regions should be kept separate.

6.   Calculate the means of your results from each region. Hence estimate the proportion of large trees on the plot.

7.   Calculate the variances of the total number of trees per area in each of your two samples. Suggest why choosing a stratified sample of 14 areas with more than 8 from Region 2 might have improved the reliability of your estimates.

Sampling scheme A used a **simple random sample.** Scheme B used a **stratified random sample,** so called because the plot was divided into two regions (strata).

15

Improving precision

Suppose that the aces are removed from an ordinary pack of cards and that the remaining cards are assigned scores as follows:

2	3	4	5	6	7	8	9	10	J	Q	K
2	3	4	5	6	7	8	9	10	10	10	10

The mean score is then $\dfrac{2 + \ldots + 9 + 4 \times 10}{12} = 7$. Knowing the actual mean score allows you to see how well various sampling schemes estimate this mean.

1. Shuffle the pack and take two cards at random. Calculate the mean of your sample. This will be an estimate of the actual mean score, 7.

2. Replacing the cards between samples, repeat the method used in question 1 until you have twenty estimates of the actual mean score. Plot a simple stick graph of these estimates like the example below.

3. Now suppose the pack is split into two, with all the cards which score 7 or less in one pack (stratum) and all the cards of score more than 7 in the other pack. Shuffle both packs and select one card from each pack. Calculate the mean of your sample of two cards.

4. Repeat the sampling method used in question 3 until you have twenty estimates of the actual mean score. Compare a simple stick graph of these estimates with the one obtained in question 2. Which sampling method appears to have greater precision?

5E. Use a computer or calculator to investigate the effect of choosing samples of greater size and of choosing stratified samples which sample the cards up to 7 more intensely than the higher value cards.

Tutorial sheet

All the people above are involved in some form of recreational activity. Conduct a survey into people's recreational interests.

Write a report of your survey describing the decisions you made and illustrating your results. State your conclusions and any limitations of your survey.

3   *Food tasting*

3.1   Introduction

Over the last few decades, food and drink manufacturers and retail outlets have faced a variety of challenges. For example, as people have become more health conscious, phrases such as 'contains no artificial flavourings' and 'with added fibre' have begun to appear on packaging. However, people seem unwilling to eat something which is better for them unless it tastes at least as good as the original product!

Launching a new or improved product can be very expensive, so before it is brought onto the market, a manufacturer needs evidence that customers will buy it. Suppose you are considering whether to market a new type of chicken product. Before you test whether people like the taste of your product, you may conduct a preliminary survey to see if there is a demand for a new food item of this kind.

If you come to the conclusion that there is sufficient demand for you to launch your new product, then you want to be sure that it will sell. In this section and the next, you will set up taste testing **experiments** to see if people can detect a difference in taste between two very similar products. In such an experiment you do not collect existing data as you do in a survey but new data which result from the experiment. The experiments you carry out only use a small sample of people. Such an experiment is called a pilot study and, after the pilot study has been completed, you could go on to conduct a full study using a larger sample of tasters.

(a)   **Describe some of the information you would be interested in collecting in the preliminary survey.**

(b)   **In what ways can a pilot study help you design a larger experiment?**

3.2 The triangle test

Various types of test have been designed to measure to what extent, if at all, a taster is able to detect a difference in taste between two products. One particular test is called the **triangle test.**

> **A triangle test measures the ability to distinguish between two products. In the test, each taster is presented with three samples, two of product A and one of product B. The taster has to determine which is the odd one out. Each trial is repeated a number of times.**

   TASKSHEET 1 – *The triangle test*

The results from a triangle test can be analysed using the binomial distribution, as in the next example.

Example 1

A triangle test was conducted to see if people can tell the difference between white turkey meat and chicken. Each of 10 people was given two samples of chicken and one of turkey in random order and asked to choose the odd one out. Assuming that there is no detectable difference in taste, what is the probability that 7 or more people would choose correctly?

Solution

Assuming that there is no detectable difference, let X be the number of times the turkey sample is chosen as the odd one out. Then X is a binomial distribution with $n = 10$ and $p = \dfrac{1}{3}$.

$$P(X \geq 7) = P(X = 7) + P(X = 8) + P(X = 9) + P(X = 10)$$

$$= \binom{10}{7}\left(\frac{1}{3}\right)^{7}\left(\frac{2}{3}\right)^{3} + \binom{10}{8}\left(\frac{1}{3}\right)^{8}\left(\frac{2}{3}\right)^{2} + \binom{10}{9}\left(\frac{1}{3}\right)^{9}\left(\frac{2}{3}\right)^{1} + \binom{10}{10}\left(\frac{1}{3}\right)^{10}\left(\frac{2}{3}\right)^{0}$$

$$\approx 0.019$$

> **Suppose that in the actual triangle test, 7 people choose correctly. Would you decide that people can detect a difference in taste? Justify your answer.**

3.3   The duo-trio test

The **duo-trio** test can be used as an alternative to the triangle test.

> In a *duo-trio* test, each taster is presented with three samples, the first one of which is stated to be the reference sample. One of the further two samples matches the reference sample and the other is a sample of a similar tasting product. The taster has to decide which of the two matches the reference sample.

TASKSHEET 2 – *The duo-trio test*

Example 2

A duo-trio test was conducted to see whether people can detect a difference in taste between lemonade and diet lemonade. 12 tasters took part in the experiment. Each taster was given a sample of ordinary lemonade as a reference sample. He or she then tasted two further samples in random order, one of lemonade and one of diet lemonade and stated which matched the reference sample. 9 tasters were correct. Would you conclude that people can tell the difference between lemonade and diet lemonade?

Solution

Assuming that there is no detectable difference in taste, then the number, X, of correct identifications would have a binomial distribution with $n = 12$ and $p = \frac{1}{2}$.

$$P(X \geq 9) = P(X = 9) + P(X = 10) + P(X = 11) + P(X = 12)$$

$$= \binom{12}{9}\left(\frac{1}{2}\right)^{12} + \binom{12}{10}\left(\frac{1}{2}\right)^{12} + \binom{12}{11}\left(\frac{1}{2}\right)^{12} + \binom{12}{12}\left(\frac{1}{2}\right)^{12}$$

$$\approx 0.073$$

On the assumption that people cannot tell the difference, the probability of as many as 9 (or more) people guessing correctly is only about 7%. It does, therefore, seem very likely that there is a detectable difference.

Example 2 provides a good summary of how to state conclusions using results calculated on the basis of an initial assumption.

> In a duo-trio test to see if people can detect a difference in taste between butter and Supaspread, 8 out of the 12 people tested correctly identified the matching sample. What would you deduce from this result?

In carrying out the experiments of Tasksheets 1 and 2, you have seen the importance of experimental design. In particular, you have seen the need to prevent bias by using random choice or a balanced design.

A balanced design is one which ensures that all possible sequences of the products being sampled occur equally often in the experiment. For example, the four sequences:

A A B

A B A

B A B

B A A

provide a basis for a duo-trio test. A balanced design for a duo-trio test with 12 tasters could use three of each sequence. The sequences can then be randomly assigned to the 12 tasters to introduce some variability, but any such experiment will always be balanced. For example, the two products will always occur equally often as the reference sample.

You should check the design of your own experiment on Tasksheet 2 and decide if there were any possible sources of bias which a modified design might have been able to eliminate. You should also analyse the results of your experiment by the method given in Example 2.

3.4   Expressing a preference

So far, you have considered tests designed to see if tasters can **detect** a difference between two products. What is often even more important is to determine which product, if any, is generally preferred.

> In a *pairs difference test*, two products are compared to see if the tasters express a preference for one of them.
>
> Each taster is given one sample of each product and states a preference. The taster may also be asked to state a reason for that preference.

TASKSHEET 3 – *The pairs difference test*

Suppose that 10 panelists have been asked which sample of peanuts (A or B) they prefer. A simple pairs difference test might produce results such as those below.

Panelist	Order	Preference
4	A then B	A
7	B then A	A
1	A then B	A
9	B then A	A
2	A then B	A
10	B then A	B
8	A then B	A
5	B then A	A
3	A then B	A
6	B then A	A

(a)   **Judging from the layout of the results above, explain how the test has been designed to eliminate possible sources of bias.**

(b)   **Assuming that people have no real preference for A or B, find the probability of A being chosen by 9 or more panelists out of 10. What would you deduce from the results above?**

(c)   **Use the results of the pairs difference test you carried out on Tasksheet 3 to decide if people have a preference between the two products you chose.**

In practice, a test to decide if people can distinguish between two products is often combined with a preference test. Combining the tests in this way saves time and is much more efficient. For example, a suitable form for a combination of a triangle test and preference test might be as shown below.

Name _____ Test number _____

Two of the three samples you have to taste are the same and one is different (odd).

1.   Write down the number of the odd sample.   ☐

2.   Tick the appropriate box.

             I prefer the odd sample.   ☐

             I prefer the others.   ☐

3.   State any reasons for your preference or other comments.

        _____

        _____

        _____

Describe some of the main features of the form above .

After working through this chapter you should:

1.   appreciate that there is a difference between carrying out a survey and conducting an experiment;

2.   be able to carry out a triangle test to see if there is a detectable difference in taste between two products;

3.   be able to carry out a duo-trio test to see if there is a detectable difference in taste between two products;

4.   be able to carry out a pairs difference test to see if people prefer the taste of one product to that of another product;

5.   understand the importance of test design and the value of a balanced design.

The triangle test

You will need to choose two similar products and then use a triangle test with approximately 12 tasters. Before starting your own experiment, you should consider the following points concerning experimental design.

- Each taster is given three samples, two of which are same. All three samples must **look** exactly the same. For example, if you are comparing decaffeinated and ordinary coffee you must put equal amounts of coffee into cups of the same size. You must also ensure that other factors such as the temperatures are identical.

- You must be able to distinguish the samples, perhaps by labelling the cups 1, 2 and 3. The taster then has simply to note the number of the sample he or she believes to be the odd one out.

- For each test, you must decide which of the products is to be duplicated.

- An important aspect of the design concerns how the order in which the tester tastes the samples is decided. It may be easier to detect differences one way round than the other.

1. Decide upon an appropriate design for your experiment. In particular, describe and justify how you intend to choose the duplicated product and how you would determine the order of tasting of the samples.

2. Design a suitable form on which to collect your results.

3. Carry out the experiment and consider whether any improvements to the procedure are necessary.

The duo-trio test

You will need to choose two similar products and then use a duo-trio test with approximately 12 tasters. Before starting your own experiment, you should consider the following points concerning experiment design.

- A duo-trio test uses three samples, two of which are the same. All three samples must **look** exactly the same. For example, if you are comparing mineral and tap water you must put equal quantities of liquid into glasses of the same size.

- You must be able to distinguish the samples. You might, for example, label as A and B the two samples being compared with the reference sample.

- The first sample given to the taster is the reference sample and this must be the same as one of the remaining two samples. You must decide whether to always use the same product for the reference sample. If not, you must decide which product is to be the reference sample for a particular taster.

- After the reference sample has been tasted, the other two samples have to be tested. An important aspect of the design concerns the order in which these two samples are presented to the taster. Even if the taster chooses the order for him or herself, the way in which the samples are placed on the table may affect this choice.

1. Decide upon an appropriate design for your experiment. In particular, describe and justify how you intend to choose the reference sample and the order of tasting for the other two samples.

2. Design a suitable form on which to collect your results.

3. Carry out the experiment and consider whether any improvements to the procedure are necessary.

The pairs difference test

You will need to choose two similar products and then use a pairs difference test to conduct an experiment to see which of the two products is preferred.

The design of a pairs difference test is especially important because the order in which people taste two products may strongly affect their decision as to a preference. For example, if one product is very slightly sweeter than the other and is tasted first, then it may make the second product appear bland and less tasty.

Design your experiment and draw up forms for the tasters to complete and a form on which you can summarise their results. You must decide whether the tasters' forms should include space for additional information such as strength of preference.

Complete the experiment and write a full report. Assuming that your experiment is a pilot study, explain fully how you would amend the design before carrying out a larger study.

Tutorial sheet

1. Ruth says she can always tell if a cup of tea had milk in first or milk added last. Briefly describe how you would test her claim.

2. An advertisement for a certain brand of cat food used to state that '$x\%$ of cat owners say their cats prefer it'. Later this was changed to '$y\%$ of cat owners who expressed a preference, say their cats prefer it'. Explain the difference between these two statements.

3. A triangle test was conducted to see if people can tell the difference between the taste of 'free-range' and 'factory' reared chickens.

    (a) 6 people out of 8 chose correctly. Calculate the probability of this event or a more extreme one happening by chance. Do you think this provides evidence that people can distinguish the two types?

    (b) Does the information provided suggest 'free-range' chickens taste better than 'factory' chickens?

4. In a duo-trio test, 16 people were asked if they could detect a difference in taste between butter and margarine.

    (a) Briefly describe how this could be done and note any special precautions that should be taken.

    (b) 12 of the people chose correctly. Does this suggest a detectable difference in taste? Provide the necessary calculations to support your statement.

5. The following results are from a simple pairs difference study. 8 people were asked if they preferred 'new recipe' crisps to the 'original' version. The results were as follows:

Tester	Order	Preference
3	N then O	N
1	O then N	O
7	N then O	N
5	O then N	N
4	N then O	O
8	O then N	N
2	N then O	O
6	O then N	N

N = 'new recipe'
O = 'original'

    (a) Assuming that people have no preference for either variety, explain why X, the number who express a preference for the new variety, has distribution $B(8, \frac{1}{2})$.

    (b) Calculate the probability of the given outcome or a more extreme one.

28

4 Testing drugs

4.1 Clinical trials

When a new drug is discovered it must be tested rigorously before it can be released for general use. It is first tested for toxicity and then an initial trial involving a small number of people is carried out. Next, there is a full-scale investigation of its effects involving more patients or volunteers. Further trials take place after the drug has been released onto the market.

Statistics play an important part in the design and analysis of experiments which are carried out to investigate the effects and effectiveness of drugs. Such experiments are called clinical trials. In this chapter you will simulate the design of a clinical trial involving a fictitious new drug, B12546.

New drug to tackle heart disease

by Staff Reporter
Peter Driver

Hypertension (high blood pressure) can cause heart attacks, heart disease and strokes. Sufferers from hypertension have been given hope by news of a new drug, B12546.

The drug company ACE Pharmaceuticals have published satisfactory results from toxicity tests at their laboratories in New Malden. Consultant Geraldine Matthews will now be able to start administering the drug in special trials at Eastleigh Royal Hospital. It is hoped that the drug will soon be generally available.

Dr. Matthews spoke yesterday of the potential advantages of B12546. Improvements in blood pressure can be expected within a week of taking the drug. In the long term, it is hoped that regular treatment with B12546 will enable sufferers to look forward to a much healthier future.

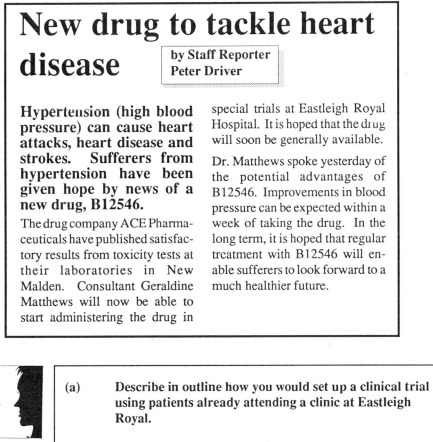

(a) **Describe in outline how you would set up a clinical trial using patients already attending a clinic at Eastleigh Royal.**

(b) **How would you try to ensure that any benefits or side-effects can be attributed to the use of B12546?**

(c) **Describe some of the ethical problems which might affect the design of this clinical trial.**

4.2   Choosing treatment groups

At the beginning of a clinical trial, several measurements (called the **baseline** measurements) are recorded for each of the patients. For a study of hypertension, the data would include measurements of blood pressure and also of various **factors** which may be significant, such as age and weight. It is then usual to divide the patients into two groups. One group takes the new course of treatment while the other group, called the **control** group, takes either the standard treatment or a placebo. How patients are allocated to the two groups is an important aspect of experiment design. Two of the main methods are considered on Tasksheet 1.

   TASKSHEET 1 – *Allocating treatments*

Two alternative methods for choosing the treatment and control groups are as follows.

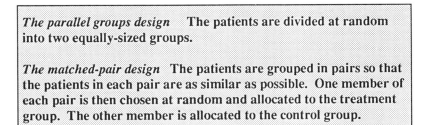

The parallel groups design   The patients are divided at random into two equally-sized groups.

The matched-pair design   The patients are grouped in pairs so that the patients in each pair are as similar as possible. One member of each pair is then chosen at random and allocated to the treatment group. The other member is allocated to the control group.

The aim of both methods is to remove any bias and thereby ensure that any results can be attributed to the differences in treatment of the two groups.

Bias can be introduced when the patients and/or doctors know who is getting which treatment. A particular example of this is when patients volunteer for a new treatment. It has been found that volunteers generally have a better chance of recovery than others. In many experiments, both doctors and patients are unaware of how patients have been allocated to the control and treatment groups.

In an open trial, both doctor and patient know which treatment is being used.

In a single blind trial, only the doctor knows which patients are receiving which treatment.

In a double blind trial, neither doctor nor patient knows which treatment is being used.

Blind trials raise important ethical issues. Ethics committees are set up to prevent the exposure of patients to unjustifiable risks, the wasting of time and money and the publication of misleading trial results. Before a trial takes place, a protocol has to be prepared giving details of the experimental design and how the data will be analysed.

4.3   Analysing the data

Clinical trials often produce a large amount of data. The results of a trial may even show that other variables need to be studied and this will sometimes lead to further trials.

Various statistical tests have been designed to analyse data from trials and some of these are described in other units of the *16-19 Mathematics* course. A simple analysis of results from a parallel groups trial is considered on Tasksheet 2.

   TASKSHEET 2 – *Analysis*

The results from an experiment usually give rise to data concerning the change in some important variable, called the **response variable**. In the case of B12546, the response variable was diastolic blood pressure.

The witticism that 'with medical attention flu can be cured in seven days – without treatment it will drag on for a week', illustrates the need to compare the results for the treatment group with the results for the control group.

> **A successful trial of a drug requires the treatment group to show significantly better changes in the response variable than occur in either the control group or with standard treatments. Furthermore, the trial must demonstrate no serious side-effects.**

The **significance** of the results depends upon how carefully controlled other factors have been and also depends upon the size of the trial. In practice, it may not be feasible to have a large sample of patients. Indeed, the sample is often drawn from such a restricted population that results cannot automatically be assumed to apply to the population of all potential users of the treatment.

The results from Tasksheet 2 were from a parallel groups trial. You have already seen that a matched-pair design has considerable advantages in reducing the effects of factors other than the actual treatment. However, it is not always easy to set up a matched-pair test and a couple of alternatives are considered in the final section of this chapter.

4.4   Other experimental designs

If parallel groups are used then it may be difficult to assess to what extent differences in the response variable are due to the treatment and to what extent they are caused by random differences between the two groups of people. The matched-pair design is especially useful when the people in each pair are as similar as possible. Many animal experiments use pairs of genetically identical animals from the same litter. Variations between the experimental group and the control group are therefore minimal.

> **Which human beings are ideal for matched-pair experiments?**

One way to minimise variations between the experimental group and the control group is to use the **same** people in each group! Such an experiment is called a **crossover trial.**

> **In a crossover trial, each patient receives both treatments in random order.**

The appropriateness of a crossover trial critically depends upon whether the first trial will significantly affect the second one. A crossover design would be particularly inappropriate if patients were cured by the first treatment! When drugs are used in a crossover trial, there must be a 'wash-out' period between the two treatments to eliminate any carry-over effects.

A further important aspect of crossover trials is that they take at least twice as long as an equivalent parallel groups experiment. They are therefore only appropriate for experiments of relatively short duration. In particular, they cannot be used in experiments designed to consider the long-term effects of various treatments.

> **Suppose you were investigating the effect of various forms of exercise on pulse-rate. What are the advantages and disadvantages of using a crossover design for the trial?**

So far in this section, you have considered some special cases of matched-pair design. In practice, it can be very difficult to form the people available for a trial into closely matched pairs. Instead of separating the patients into pairs you can consider separating them into groups or blocks, each block consisting of patients with similar characteristics.

```
• • • • • • • • • • • • • • • • • • • • • • • • • • • • • • • •
•                                                              •
•   • MIGRAINE RELIEF                                          •
•                                                              •
•   There's a rosier future in store for migraine sufferers    •
•   whose attacks are triggered by fluorescent lights, because •
•   rose-tinted glasses may help to combat the problem.  De-   •
•   veloped by Dr Arnold Wilkins at the Medical Research       •
•   Council's  Applied Psychology Unit and Cambridge Op-       •
•   tical, spectacles fitted with special lenses were tested on •
•   20 schoolchildren who suffered from migraines, and 60      •
•   volunteer office staff working on VDUs under fluorescent   •
•   lighting. The children's migraines were reduced by about   •
•   74% and the adults reported a 38% drop in headaches and    •
•   eyestrain.                                                 •
•       Dr Wilkins also advises migraine sufferers to swap     •
•   conventional fluorescent lights for the newer 'nonflicker' •
•   varieties that oscillate more than 30,000 times per second •
•   – too fast for the brain to register, or to provoke a migraine. •
•                                                              •
• • • • • • • • • • • • • • • • • • • • • • • • • • • • • • • •
```

Good Housekeeping February 1992

One problem with the experiment described in the article above is that the trial appears to have had no control. The important experimental design called **permuted block design** combines the idea of using blocks with the use of a control group.

> A *permuted block design* involves grouping the patients into a number of blocks, each containing an even number of patients with similar characteristics. The people in each block are then evenly allocated, at random, into the treatment group and the control group.

> (a)   Describe how the experiment on the use of rose-tinted spectacles could have been set up using a permuted block design.
>
> (b)   Compare your design with the one described in the article.

An advantage of using blocks is that you can investigate the results from each block separately as well as obtain information about the sample as a whole. Any results can then be used in a similar way to results from a stratified survey. For example, the value of a treatment for 'middle-aged males who smoke' would be estimated from results for a block of patients with the same characteristics.

After working through this chapter you should:

1.	be aware that statistical ideas and ethical considerations are both important in the design of experiments;

2.	understand why placebos are used in trials;

3.	know what is meant by an open trial and by a blind trial;

4.	understand the use of a control group;

5.	appreciate the need to minimise bias and the effect of random variations;

6.	know what is meant by the following types of experimental design:

	•	parallel groups
	•	matched-pair
	•	crossover
	•	permuted block.

Allocating treatments

Suppose that 16 male hypertensive patients are available to take part in a trial of B12546 and that their baseline data for certain key factors are as shown:

Patient No.	Age (years)	Weight (kg)	Smoker/ Non-smoker
1	57	98.6	N
2	45	99.6	N
3	40	100.1	N
4	63	80.9	N
5	23	81.3	S
6	33	82.1	S
7	50	67.8	N
8	47	80.5	S
9	40	69.9	S
10	40	86.7	N
11	54	118.5	N
12	58	84.3	S
13	70	80.1	N
14	38	81.8	S
15	46	70.3	N
16	52	81.0	S

The patients are to be divided into two groups, A and B. Patients in one of the groups will receive B12546, whereas patients in the other group will receive a placebo.

1.   Allocate each patient either to group A or to group B at random, for example by tossing a coin. What is likely to be a major disadvantage of this method of allocation?

Parallel groups design

2.   Randomly divide the 16 patients into two groups of 8. Find the mean and variance of the ages and weights for your two groups. How similar are they with respect to their baseline measurements?

Matched-pair design

3.   Group the patients into 8 pairs so that the patients in each pair are as similar as possible with respect to their baseline variables. Explain carefully the procedure you have used.

4.   Randomly allocate one member of each pair to group A and the other member to group B. How similar are your two treatment groups?

5.   What advantages does a matched-pair design have over a parallel groups design?

Analysis

Blood pressure which is measured when the heart is dilating is called diastolic blood pressure. This pressure is measured in millimetres of mercury. Suppose a parallel groups trial of B12546 was limited to 16 male patients whose original diastolic blood pressures (when hypertension was first diagnosed) were between 105 and 115 mm.

The table gives the blood pressures at the end of the third week of the trial (before treatment) and at the end of the fourth week of the trial (after treatment). Group A received B12546 and group B received a placebo.

Patient No.	Group	Diastolic blood pressure (mm)	
		after three weeks	after four weeks
1	A	120	100
2	B	110	105
3	A	105	90
4	A	106	90
5	B	85	90
6	A	70	80
7	B	110	100
8	B	100	100
9	A	100	90
10	B	82	90
11	A	103	95
12	B	88	95
13	A	100	75
14	B	105	95
15	A	100	100
16	B	95	100

1.　(a)　The blood pressures were taken after the patients had been lying down for 15 minutes. What was the purpose of this aspect of the experimental design?

　　(b)　Why did treatment start after three weeks of the trial?

2.　Find the mean and variance of blood pressures before and after treatment for each group. What simple measure can be used to compare the effects of treatments A and B?

3.　Design a table or tables to display the data given above in such a way as to enable a simple visual comparison to be made between the two treatments.

4.　What conclusion can you draw from this experiment? In particular, to what population do your conclusions apply?

Tutorial sheet

A new drug to prevent sea-sickness, C184, is to be compared with the standard cure, *Staywell*, in a trial involving passengers on the Fjord line between Larvik and Newcastle. All passengers who normally suffer from sea-sickness are being invited to take part in a double-blind trial.

1.   On August 5th, 100 passengers on the 4 a.m. ferry from Larvik to Newcastle volunteer to take part. Only 25 are needed for each of the two treatments in a parallel groups test.

    (a)   Explain how the two groups of patients can be formed using random digits.

    (b)   Why is it necessary for one group of patients to be given *Staywell*?

    (c)   Explain why a double-blind trial is being used.

    (d)   What problems might there be with the results of this trial?

2.   On September 3rd, 80 passengers on the 1 p.m. ferry from Newcastle to Larvik volunteer. All 80 volunteers are asked to fill in a questionnaire and 25 closely matched pairs are selected.

    (a)   Suggest some of the questions that might be asked to identify 25 matched pairs.

    (b)   Explain how the volunteers would be allocated treatments.

    (c)   Why is this a better design than that used in question 1?

3.   50 volunteers on the 4 a.m. ferry from Larvik on October 10th and who will be returning to Norway by the same route are chosen to take part in a trial. They are formed into two groups of 25. One group takes C184 on the outward journey and *Staywell* on the return journey. The other group takes *Staywell* on the outward journey and C184 on the return journey. Explain some of the problems with this crossover design.

5 *Summary*

5.1 Statistical activity

A statistical study encompasses four main activities.

- Deciding on the objective(s)

- Collecting appropriate data

- Analysing the data

- Interpreting the results

None of these activities can be treated in total isolation from the others. Precisely what your objectives are will affect the whole design of your study, your analysis will only be successful if the data itself is appropriate and the interpretation of your results may well affect the objectives of future statistical studies.

The stage of setting the objectives for a statistical study of your own should be given careful attention. For example, the objectives of determining if people can 'distinguish butter from margarine' and determining if people 'prefer butter to margarine' lead to different experiments. You must therefore take care to set a precise objective and, in the example just described, it would also be necessary to be clear what you will mean by 'people', 'butter' and 'margarine'.

Unlike many books on statistics, this unit has concentrated not on analysis but on the other statistical activities and, especially, on the collection of data. This chapter reviews some of the ideas you have met and sets them in the context of general ideas common to all data collection.

It is hoped that your work on this unit, together with the experience of carrying out your own surveys and experiments, will have raised your awareness of some of the issues involved in the business of collecting data. The next time you hear the result of a survey or a trial stated in the form '7 out of 10 cats prefer ... ', you should find yourself wondering 'How was that result obtained?'

5.2   An overview of sampling

The following terminology can be applied to any sampling procedure.

Population   The set of all possible observations. For example, the diameters of
                all the trees in a forest.

Census   A collection of data for the whole population.

Sample   A collection of data from a subset of the population.

Statistic   A single numerical fact obtained from a sample. For example, the
                mean diameter of the sampled trees.

Parameter   A single numerical fact for the whole population. For example, the
                mean diameter of all the trees in the forest.

The general purpose of sampling is to estimate the value of a parameter from the value
of the corresponding statistic. The parameter could be found directly using a census.
However, this is often too expensive or time consuming and for many experiments it
would be impossible.

Precision   The precision of a sampling procedure is a measure of how good an
                estimate of the parameter the sample is likely to provide.

Sampling units   The 'objects' which are to be sampled. In the forest survey these
                could have been the individual trees but you actually sampled
                collections of trees, the 168 sampling areas.

Sampling frame   A list of all the sampling units. Random sampling requires a
                sampling frame so that each sampling unit can be given an equal
                chance of selection. If you had to conduct a survey of people who
                walk to work, you would find it impossible to obtain a sampling
                frame and so you would not be able to use random sampling.

The above definitions apply to both surveys and experiments. In experiments, the term
'experimental unit' is generally used instead of 'sampling unit'.

5.3   Replication

In the forest survey, the sampling areas contain different numbers of trees and different proportions of large trees. If a statistic was based upon just one sampling area, then it would be unlikely to be a good estimate for the corresponding parameter. It is therefore usual to repeat or replicate your calculations in a number of sampling areas.

If you considered **every** sampling area, then your estimate would be precise. You might therefore expect that increasing the sample size is likely to improve the precision of any sampling procedure. As well as seeming to be simple common sense, this can be proved mathematically. In deciding how large a sample you need, you must bear in mind a number of factors.

- **Variability**   In some situations it is possible to calculate the likely error in a statistic. This so called **sampling error** is studied in some of the other *16-19 Mathematics* units. As a general rule, the more variable the data you have collected, then the more observations you need before you can have any confidence in your estimate. For this reason, it was recommended that you should sample more heavily from the more variable strata in a stratified survey.

- **Cost**   Data collection is expensive and time consuming. There is therefore no point in collecting more data once estimates of sufficient precision have been found.

- **Purpose**   It is unlikely that anyone would need to know the precise number of trees in a forest. Given that you will estimate the amount of timber from each tree, an estimate of the number of trees is all that would be needed. Indeed, the results of census might well be unreliable because of the likelihood of errors in such a massive undertaking.

- **Time**   In a clinical trial, the size of the experiment and the time taken to carry it out are important apart from any financial costs involved. The quicker the experiment is completed, the sooner a potentially valuable drug will be available for general use. Conversely, if a drug has dangerous side effects, it is important to discover this quickly with as few people as possible being exposed to any risks.

5.4   Randomisation

There is considerable danger of your results being biased if you select sample members or allocate treatments in an opportunistic way. For example, consider the following selection methods for two situations you have already met.

(a)   Give the drug C184 to the first 30 passengers to volunteer, give *Staywell* to the next 30 volunteers.

(b)   Walk through the forest and choose 14 sampling areas evenly spaced along your route.

> **Comment on the appropriateness or otherwise of the selection methods (a) and (b)**

A random selection cannot be made haphazardly. Considerable care must be taken in selecting a sample of size *n* if each possible set of *n* sampling units is to be equally likely to be chosen.

> **Random selection is an important feature of both experiments and surveys.**

How you perform the random selection may depend upon your access to technology. For small samples, simple devices such as coins, dice and playing cards can be much easier to use than either random number tables or random number generators. For example:

•   To decide on the allocation of a treatment and placebo to members of a matched pair, simply toss a coin;

•   Suppose that you have formed a block containing 8 members of a population with similar characteristics. To form a random permuted block with the members separated evenly into two groups, A and B, simply shuffle a pack of 8 playing cards, 4 red and 4 black. Deal the cards face up in a line and allocate members of the block to the two groups according to whether the corresponding card is red or black.

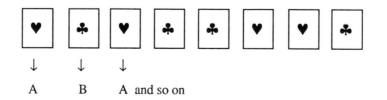

SOLUTIONS

1 *Data and inference*

1.1   Data, data everywhere!

> **Comment on the 'design' of this survey.**

This is an interesting way of collecting information and it is almost certainly the case that had those buying the books been asked directly (perhaps one month after the purchase) if they had read the book, the conclusions might have been different! The designers had taken a number of precautions (hiding the coupon, paying money to callers, allowing sufficient time for them to telephone) so why was there such a low response?

Some points which should be made about this survey are as follows.

*   This was not actually a survey to see if people read the books but if they read them within a month.

*   In the family expenditure survey of 1967, payment was made for co-operation on the part of a household and yet 29% did not respond. There are other examples of non-response for national surveys involving payment to respondents. It is therefore not clear whether most people did not read the books within a month or whether they read them but did not bother to claim the £5.

Ethical questions may arise in the collection of data and statisticians must always be conscious of their responsibilities. You will meet this important idea again in Chapter 4 when considering the design of medical experiments.

2 Survey methods

2.2 A forest survey

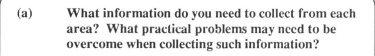

> **(a)** **What information do you need to collect from each area? What practical problems may need to be overcome when collecting such information?**
>
> **(b)** **Will 14 of the areas prove sufficient for the sample?**

(a) For each area you must obtain the number of trees and the number of large trees. A quick and easy method is needed to define what is meant by 'large' – a common method is to use a special tape to measure the diameter of the tree at chest height. It is conventional to describe a pine with a diameter of more than 30 cm as large. The Forestry Commission plants all of its commercial forests in straight lines and so counting is relatively easy.

The 14 areas must be chosen at random. You might, for example, number each area and use random numbers to select 14 numbers from 1 to 168.

(b) Without some experience of similar sampling exercises, you cannot tell whether a sample of 14 areas will be sufficient. Organisations conducting sampling procedures usually have a clear idea of the reliability of their estimates.

2.3 Choosing a stratified sample

> **Describe how you might choose the strata in a survey to estimate the amount of money per week spent on entertainment by 16-19 year olds.**

Your first task in any such survey would be to define precisely what counts as 'entertainment'. Some important ways of dividing the population into strata whose spending behaviours are likely to differ greatly are as follows:

• by gender;

• by whether or not the person lives at home;

• by whether the person is employed, unemployed or a student.

You may have thought of several other good ways of stratifying the population.

> **Suppose you have to predict the support for the various politi-
> cal parties in a forthcoming general election. Suppose further
> that the electorate has been divided into strata according to
> age and profession. Explain why it might be appropriate to
> sample more heavily from the young and from white collar
> workers.**

The voting behaviour of many people is reasonably stable. Consequently, it is important to focus attention on new voters and those who are prone to change allegiance (the
'floating' voters).

At each general election, those eligible to vote for the first time can span up to 5 years
of the age range of the population. This stratum therefore comprises a large number of
people whose voting intentions (and indeed whether they vote at all) can significantly
affect the result. Whilst the connection between party allegiance and social class is far
from straightforward, the simple division between 'working-class' and 'middle-class'
still provides probably the clearest division of the electorate into strata with dissimilar
voting intentions. The growth in the numbers of white collar workers is one of the
major factors which blurs this distinction and so the intentions of this stratum have
special importance.

Focussing on various strata of the electorate whose intentions you believe to be more
volatile is just one example of the use of stratified sampling. A similar idea is employed when pollsters concentrate on the key marginals – those constituencies which
are most likely to change hands.

2.4 Questionnaire design

> **How would you stratify for the National Food Survey?**

You might stratify on:

Socio-economic class	People with different backgrounds may have different eating habits.
Income	Those with higher incomes may or may not spend more on food and buy different sorts of food.
Age distribution of children	Families with very young children might buy baby food, for example.
Geographical region	Eating habits are different in different regions.
Rural/non-rural area	Families in rural areas may eat more fresh farm produce. They may also eat more frozen food as they may not visit a supermarket as often as those who live in towns.

> Describe some of the design features in the following extract of a questionnaire on milk consumption.

Some of the features you may have commented on are as follows:

- The questionnaire starts with a brief and simple explanation of the purpose of the research in a way which will encourage the respondent to take the time to complete the form.

- Respondents are directed away from questions (like numbers 4 and 5) if they are not relevant.

- The questions are intended to be clearly worded and simple to answer.

- A very important feature is the way respondents only need to tick boxes. This idea is covered in more depth in the next thinking point.

> (a)   What would be an open response question format for question 2?
>
> (b)   Suggest some of the advantages and disadvantages of open response questions. What are the advantages and disadvantages of closed response questions?
>
> (c)   Discuss the actual format of question 2 in the light of your answers to (b).

(a)   'Where do you usually buy milk?'

(b)   **Open response**

Some advantages are:

- respondents think more deeply about their answers;
- information may become available which the interviewer had not anticipated.

Some disadvantages are:

- an interviewer has to decide whether to record everything said, record relevant remarks or paraphrase the answers;
- an interviewer's interpretation of an answer may introduce bias;
- answers have to be encoded before the data can be analysed;
- respondents may find the task so time-consuming that they fail to complete the questionnaire.

Closed response

Some advantages are:

- it is simple to answer such a question;
- little thought or analysis is needed by the respondent.

Some disadvantages are:

- answers may be forced into categories in which they do not really belong;
- a reply may be wrongly recorded by ticking the wrong box;
- respondents do not think deeply enough about their replies but may just tick a box. (Some questionnaires are designed with questions repeated using a different form of words. This provides a check on whether a respondent's answers are reliable.)

(c)   Question 2 has been designed to be 'closed response' and simple to answer for most respondents. Notice also that the possibility of 'one or more' ticks has been highlighted.

Less common answers are catered for by allowing an 'open response' answer if necessary.

> **Describe some of the advantages and disadvantages of telephone sampling.**

Advantages

- Results can be obtained very quickly.

- It is especially suitable if the questions are simple and straightforward and do not require much thought.

Disadvantages

- Bias has immediately been introduced because not everyone has a telephone.

- Special care must be taken regarding who is allowed to answer the questions. The person in whose name the telephone is registered is very often male.

2.5   Opinion polls

> **Suggest possible reasons for the incorrect predictions of the polls in 1970.**

There are many possible explanations for the incorrect predictions. Apart from the fact that all polls provide only an **estimate** of the actual voting intentions, the most accepted explanation is that voting intentions can be extremely volatile in the last few weeks before an election and so the polls may have been reasonably correct at the time they were conducted.

One example of the way polls are not able to take into account all the factors just before the election itself concerns the weather on election day. This can have considerable effect on those who are undecided whether to vote or not and who form an important substratum of the 'floating voters'.

3 *Food tasting*

3.2 The triangle test

> **Suppose that in the actual triangle test, 7 people choose
> correctly. Would you decide that people can detect a
> difference in taste? Justify your answer.**

Assuming that people cannot detect a difference in taste, the chance of obtaining a
result at least as extreme as 7 out of 10 correct guesses is less than 2%. It seems very
likely that people **can** distinguish between white turkey meat and chicken.

3.3 The duo-trio test

> **In a duo-trio test to see if people can detect a difference
> in taste between butter and Supaspread, 8 out of the 12
> people tested correctly identified the matching sample.
> What would you deduce from this result?**

Assuming that people cannot detect a difference, let X be the number of correct guesses
in the test.

$$P(X \geq 8) = \binom{12}{8} \left(\frac{1}{2}\right)^{12} + P(X \geq 9)$$

$$= \binom{12}{8} \left(\frac{1}{2}\right)^{12} + 0.073$$

$$\approx 0.194$$

A result as extreme as 8 out of 12 correct guesses would occur by chance in roughly
one in five tests. The experiment has provided only very weak evidence for the hy-
pothesis that people can detect a difference between butter and Supaspread.

3.4 Expressing a preference

> (a)   Judging from the layout of the results above, explain how
>   the test has been designed to eliminate possible sources of
>   bias.
>
> (b)   Assuming that people have no real preference for A or B,
>   find the probability of A being chosen by 9 or more panel-
>   ists out of 10. What would you deduce from the results
>   above?
>
> (c)   Use the results of the pairs difference test you carried out
>   on Tasksheet 3 to decide if people have a preference
>   between the two products you chose.

(a)   The test appears to have a balanced design using repetitions of:

A then B
B then A

The panelists have then been allocated at random.

(b)   Suppose people are as equally likely to state a preference for A as for B. Let X be the number of people in a sample of 10 who say they prefer A. Then X has a binomial distribution with $n = 10$ and $p = \frac{1}{2}$.

$$P(X \geq 9) = P(X = 9) + P(X = 10)$$
$$= \binom{10}{9} \left(\frac{1}{2}\right)^{10} + \binom{10}{10} \left(\frac{1}{2}\right)^{10}$$
$$\approx 0.011$$

The probability of an event as extreme as 9 people choosing A by chance is approximately 1%. This is very unlikely and so the experiment provides strong evidence that A is generally preferred.

(c)   –

> **Describe some of the main features of the form above.**

The test number is important because the person setting up the experiment will need this to know which sample is the odd one out and which product this represents.

The tester's name is important for some tests but in other situations it would be inappropriate.

Questions 1 and 2 are closed. Boxes have been used to ensure that the responses will be easy to analyse.

Question 1 is used for a triangle test.

Question 2 allows for a simple pairs difference test. Sometimes a third box is used to allow people to express 'no preference'.

Question 3 is open. Once the results from questions 1 and 2 have been analysed, the responses to this question may be of use, perhaps to decide precisely what characteristics of a product should be stressed in advertising or possibly to decide what characteristics must be changed.

4 Testing drugs

4.4 Other experimental designs

> **Which human beings are ideal for matched-pair experiments?**

Identical twins are ideal for matched-pair trials. However, they are sufficiently rare for their use to be extremely limited.

A number of psychological and sociological experiments have used identical twins because the twins tend to be so similar in mental and emotional attributes as well as in physical make-up.

> **Suppose you were investigating the effect of various forms of exercise on pulse-rate. What are the advantages and disadvantages of using a crossover design for the trial?**

The responses of different people to exercise differ so greatly that, provided you allow sufficient time between spells of activity, it would be ideal to use the same sample of people for each form of exercise. However, you could not use the same people if the exercises were so strenuous that each activity had long-term effects.

> **(a)** Describe how the experiment on the use of rose-tinted spectacles could have been set up using a permuted block design.
>
> **(b)** Compare your design with the one described in the article.

(a) Perhaps the simplest design would be to divide, at random, each of the two blocks of people (office staff and children) into a treatment group and a control group. During the trial, the control group could wear ordinary tinted spectacles. All the people would be told that they were testing a possible means of preventing migraine.

A further sub-division of the blocks of people might be useful in seeing to what extent the effect of wearing the spectacles depends upon age and living and working conditions.

(b) The problem with the experiment as described in the article is that you do not know what effect (if any) came simply from being in the trial. The need for a control is strengthened by the fact that the office staff were volunteers. Treatments often have a more beneficial effect on volunteers than on people in general.

5 *Summary*

5.4   Randomisation

> **Comment on the appropriateness or otherwise of the selection methods (a) and (b)**

(a)   The first 30 volunteers may be especially eager to try out a new drug and this may predispose them to react especially well during the trial. Conversely, they may be eager because they are the most seriously affected passengers! The problem is that you cannot be sure whether or not bias is being introduced into your results and so this is a badly designed procedure.

(b)   Again, you cannot be sure whether or not bias is being introduced. Perhaps the path naturally follows a route through less densely wooded parts of the forest, perhaps there are more small trees near the path, ... , and so on.

COMMENTARIES

1 Data and inference

1.2   Survey and experiment

> A biology class proposes to investigate the effect of water
> temperature on the growth rate of tadpoles. They have 150
> tadpoles, together with a number of jars with thermostats, and
> have decided to compare temperatures of 10°C, 15°C and 20°C.
>
> Discuss the design of this investigation and consider general
> ideas that might be useful in the design of other investigations.

You might consider the following approaches:

1.   If you accept the basic design as given, i.e. 150 tadpoles and 3 different tempera-
      tures, examples of variations you could consider are:

      (a)   to use 3 jars with 50 tadpoles in each;

      (b)   to use 150 jars with 1 tadpole in each;

      (c)   to use 15 jars with 10 tadpoles in each.

      The discussion could consider general issues. For example, how many thermo-
      stats are there? How much laboratory space is there? Might tadpoles suffer from
      overcrowding in (a) or loneliness in (b)?

      More technical issues can also be mentioned. For instance, in experiment (c) what
      is the sample size? Is it 15 (jars) or 150 (tadpoles)?

      If a similar study has been conducted in previous years, there may be data avail-
      able that could help you to choose the design.

2.   You could question the basis of the study. Tadpoles do not normally live in ther-
      mostatically controlled jars in a laboratory, so how realistic is the whole study?
      Why not study tadpoles in their natural habitat?

      It is not really possible to control the temperature in a pond, but you could find a
      number of ponds with tadpoles. In each pond you could record both the growth
      rate and the temperature. Would this be better? Would there be any practical or
      conceptual problems?

In this unit, the first type of study is called an experiment, while the second is called a
survey.

Tutorial sheet

1.   (a)   On the basis of the information given, you can infer nothing about the performances of the schools. You simply have the factual information that 'on a particular test the average reading age of 11-year-olds in the school was ...'

        Some of the many factors which need to be considered before anything can be inferred about the performances of the schools are as follows.

- How reliable is this particular test?

- What were the sample sizes? (The village school might only have a few pupils.)

- Were the tests taken at the same time in the school year?

- Are the catchment areas of the two schools similar?

    (b)   First you would need to define 'performance'. There are many features of a school apart from academic performance which might be taken into account. You could, for example, use the truancy rate and the proportion of 16-year-olds staying on in your measure of performance.

        If you use academic performance as a measure, then you must consider the 'base line' abilities of the pupils. For example, if you were looking at A level success in a sixth-form college you could perhaps consider the pupils' performance in examinations at age 16 as a base line measure.

        The choice of measure is crucially important and the way you define performance will affect the inferences that you will be able to make from any figures you obtain for a school.

2.   Arguably, the main advantages are as given below. You may have thought of a number of other possibilities. Whether you use a survey or an experiment, it is important to note that weights at birth are very variable irrespective of whether or not the mothers smoke during pregnancy.

    (a)   A survey gives the opportunity to collect and analyse data from a large sample relatively quickly. (You do not have to wait during the nine months of a full-term pregnancy!)

    (b)   The purpose of the study is presumably to find out if a change in behaviour is advisable. It may therefore be particularly important to study the effect, for habitual smokers, of not smoking during pregnancy. You might therefore carry out an experiment with two groups of smokers. The members of one group are helped and encouraged to give up smoking during their pregnancies and their success in doing this must be carefully monitored.

2 *Survey methods*

2.1 Introduction

> A town planning department wishes to use a survey to discover what facilities may be required in a sports centre they intend to build. Describe how they might obtain the information and any problems they may encounter in ensuring that they have the representative views of those living in the town.

They would first need to be clear about the sort of information they require. They might want to know for example:

- who would use the centre and for what purpose;
- how regularly they would use it;
- at what times they would use it;
- how much they would be prepared to pay;
- how they would travel to the sports centre.

You doubtless can think of many other areas of interest.

To obtain valid information about requirements they would need to take care to ask people across the full age range. It would be important to record the age and sex of the respondent as this would provide useful information. Using a questionnaire would be the best way of obtaining the information – perhaps by asking people directly to answer questions rather than posting out forms.

If the sampling method used was to ask every tenth person in a shopping arcade on a Saturday afternoon then some points of view would be disproportionately represented. The whole exercise needs considerable thought and careful planning.

To the woods!

1.   You must ensure that **every** number has an equal chance of being selected. Using a computer or calculator is the easiest way of generating the numbers. Most devices have a simple means of generating a whole number from 1 to N, for any N. You must repeat this until you have obtained 14 **different** numbers.

      This straightforward method is efficient because 14 is very much smaller than 168 and so you are unlikely to need to repeat the procedure much more than 14 times.

2.   Your table should record the plot number, the numbers of small and large trees and the total number of trees on the strip.

3.   Typical results for scheme A are as shown.

Plot number	Small trees	Large trees	Total
15	74	127	201
16	78	135	213
27	71	121	192
30	78	113	191
32	107	147	254
40	85	137	222
63	86	128	214
69	91	139	230
81	100	222	322
88	90	221	311
108	110	238	348
127	107	205	312
166	104	189	293
167	107	238	345
Mean	92	168.6	260.6

The estimates are:

•   the number of trees on the whole plot is $168 \times 260.6 \approx 43\,800$;

•   the number of large trees is $168 \times 168.6 \approx 28\,300$;

•   the proportion of large trees is $\frac{28\,300}{43\,800} \approx 0.65$.

4.   6 : 8 is the same ratio as 72 : 96.

5.   Tables similar to the one for question 3 should be used.

(continued)

6. Typical results for scheme B are as shown.

Plot number	Small trees	Large trees	Total
Region 1			
23	87	134	221
48	76	122	198
56	89	144	233
57	94	136	230
71	79	123	202
72	93	149	242
Mean	86.3	134.7	221.0
Region 2			
74	91	189	280
80	95	233	328
84	106	242	348
89	107	222	329
116	94	196	290
119	121	258	379
139	100	240	340
141	105	228	333
Mean	102.4	226.0	328.4

An estimate for the total number of trees on the plot is $72 \times 221 + 96 \times 328.4 \approx 47\,400$.

A similar estimate for the number of large trees is $72 \times 134.7 + 96 \times 226 \approx 31\,400$.

The proportion is therefore $\frac{31\,400}{47\,400} \approx 0.66$.

7. For the samples above, the variances of the total number of trees on each plot are:

Region 1   259 (to 3 s.f.)
Region 2   865 (to 3 s.f.)

There is a much greater variation in the number of trees per plot in Region 2 than in Region 1. An estimate based on a sample from Region 1 is therefore likely to be more reliable than an estimate based on a sample from Region 2. It would therefore be a good idea to sample Region 2 more intensely, to produce an estimate of which one can be more confident.

If it is known that there is little variability, then repeated sampling simply provides more of the same information. To illustrate the point further, if a stratum consisted of identical elements (no variablity) then just one sample would provide the information you need.

Improving precision

1. If you choose, for example, 2♥ and K♣ then your estimate of the mean score would be $\frac{2+10}{2} = 6$. This is reasonably close to 7, although your estimate **could** be as low as 2 or as high as 10.

2. The stick graph given on the tasksheet was obtained by one of the authors. Yours is likely to be similar in that the estimates will be only loosely grouped around 7.

3. In this case, the lowest possible estimate you could have is $\frac{2+8}{2} = 5$ and the highest possible estimate is $\frac{7+10}{2} = 8.5$.

4. The following graph was obtained by one of the authors.

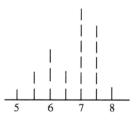

    A comparison between this stick graph and the one shown on the tasksheet suggests strongly that an estimate based upon the stratified sampling procedure is likely to have greater precision than one based upon the simple random sampling procedure. Your results (and those of others in your group) should also lead to this conclusion.

5E. The following BBC BASIC program simulates finding the average score when four cards are selected. (For simplicity, it has been assumed that each card is replaced in the pack as soon as it has been selected.) The program can easily be adapted for selection of a different number of cards or for selection from a stratum.

```
S = 0
FOR I = 1 TO 4
X = 1 + RND(12) : IF X > 10 THEN X = 10
S = S + X
NEXT I
PRINT S/4
```

    You should find that larger samples lead to greater precision, as does sampling more intensely from the stratum of low cards. Note that if you employ a stratified sampling scheme using 3 cards from the low value pack and one from the high value pack, then samples such as { 3♥, 4♠, 7♣ } and {9♦} lead to an estimate for the mean of

$$\frac{3+4+7+3\times9}{6} \approx 6.8$$

Tutorial sheet

The following aspects of reporting your survey are important.

Design

The report should convey a clear sense of purpose. You should describe precisely what you are investigating and how you intend to collect the data.

The selection of the sample and how you have avoided bias must be carefully described. If you have used a stratified sample, then you should explain the basis for your stratification and justify the sample sizes.

The design of any questionnaire is particularly important. You should describe whether or not you used a pilot survey to sort out teething problems.

Data collection and analysis

Responses should be organised and recorded so as to be amenable to analysis. The analysis itself should demonstrate an awareness of potential problems associated with data collection, for example, bias.

Interpretation/validation

Conclusions drawn from the survey results should be stated as clearly and as simply as possible. It is important to consider if you have sufficient evidence to make inferences about the recreational habits of, for example, females, students or senior citizens.

You should also decide if there were any weaknesses in your approach and, if so, how it might have been improved.

Communication/initiative

Your results must be presented in a simple and understandable way. Diagrams and tables can be very effective in improving the readability of a report.

Possible further enquiries which are suggested by the responses to your survey should be described.

3   *Food tasting*

3.1   Introduction

> **(a)** Describe some of the information you would be interested in collecting in the preliminary survey.
>
> **(b)** In what ways can a pilot study help you design a larger experiment?

(a)   The survey will enable you to collect existing data on how much chicken people buy, which strata of people buy most chicken (this will help you plan your advertising) and which products they are already buying.

(b)   •   You may obtain guidance on how to choose a sample of people.

•   The questions may prove to be misleading or ambiguous. In either case they would need to be changed.

•   Some questions may prove to be not worth asking.

•   You can see how varied the answers to open-ended questions can be.

•   You can see if you are trying to collect data in a suitable way.

•   You can see if the layout of recording forms is suitable.

•   You can test if the instructions are clear to those taking part in the experiment.

•   Terms which prove too technical can be rewritten.

•   The way in which answers to questions are encoded may need altering.

•   The order in which things are done within an experiment may need adjusting to eliminate bias.

The triangle test

FOOD TASTING

COMMENTARY

TASKSHEET 1

1. The best design is one which tries to eliminate possible bias by ensuring that each of the two products is the odd one out the same number of times and also by ensuring that the order of testing OD occurs as often as the order DO (O = Ordinary, D = Decaffeinated).

   You could either use a randomising device such as a coin to make your choices or you could use what is termed a **balanced design**. There are six possible 'orders of tasting':

   O O D
   O D O
   O D D
   D O D
   D D O
   D O O

   A balanced design would use each of these orders the same number of times. With 12 tasters you would therefore use each one of the above for two tasters.

2. A simple form might be as shown below. The tasters must not see this form!

Taster	Order of tasting	Odd one out	Choice
5	O O D	3	
12	O D O	2	
1	O D D	1	
7	D O D	2	

   A balanced design could be used for the experiment and the tasters could then be allocated at random to the various sampling orders.

3. –

The duo-trio test

1. It has been shown in past experiments that if the same product is used as the reference sample each time then the results are likely to be biased. Similarly, the two samples being tested should not always be presented in the same order.

   The best design is one in which each of the two products is used as the reference sample half the time. Similarly, each product should be equally likely to be the first sample compared with the reference sample.

   For each trial, you could toss a coin to decide which product is to be the reference sample and toss again to decide which product is tasted immediately after the reference sample.

   Alternatively, you can use a **balanced design** in which the ordering of products is determined in such a way that each product occurs equally often as the reference sample and as the first sample after the reference. Other factors may need to be balanced, for example, the number of times the reference sample and the next sample are the same and different. For this experiment, the following pattern could be repeated:

Reference sample	Order of other two samples
A	AB
A	BA
B	AB
B	BA

   A random design has the disadvantage that, by chance, bias might be introduced into a **particular** sample of 12 tastings. However, a balanced design would be unsuitable if the tasters began to suspect there was some pattern to the proceedings. This is especially important for experiments where a single taster is tested repeatedly.

2. The simplest such form would be as follows:

Reference sample	Order of other two samples	(✔ or ✗)

   As well as giving you the overall results, this format might enable you to spot patterns in correct and incorrect responses according to the ordering of the samples.

3. —

The pairs difference test

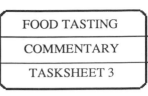

The following aspects of reporting your experiment are important.

Design

Your report must describe precisely what you are investigating and how you intend to collect the data. As well as deciding how many people and how many tastes per person you are to consider, you must decide on the overall design of the experiment.

Some form of balanced design is best. If the products are X and Y, then X and Y must be tasted first the same number of times. Your report should include a description of precautions taken to avoid obvious 'clues' such as differences in colour between the two products.

Data collection and analysis

A clear response form should be used. For example:

Name _____		Number _____
Tick **one** box for each test.		
Pair	Prefer 1st sample	Prefer 2nd sample
1	☐	☐
2	☐	☐
3	☐	☐

An appropriate analysis of results must include a statement of the model used and the basis on which calculations are made.

Interpretation/validation

Inferences should be stated simply and clearly and based on the experimental results in comparison to those predicted by the model. You should be able to make a number of criticisms of your pilot experiment and hence describe possible modifications or improvements for a future larger study.

Communication/initiative

The original collection of data should be clearly presented and tabulated/grouped as appropriate. Mathematical language and diagrams may be necessary in some parts of your report but your main conclusions must be strongly related to the original problem and stated as simply as possible.

1.   You could, for example, have 10 pairs of cups of tea. One of each pair has milk in first and the other milk in last. In 5 cases, the cup with milk in first is offered first. In the other 5 cases, the cup with milk in last is offered first.

Ruth decides which cups had milk in first. Suppose she chooses correctly in x cases. You then calculate $P(X \geq x)$ where X has a binomial distribution with $n = 10$ and $p = \frac{1}{2}$. This gives you the probability of the observed result or a more extreme one if Ruth is really guessing. If this probability is quite small it is likely that she can tell the difference.

2.   Not all cats would have shown a preference. Some cats may not mind a difference in taste between different brands or may not be able to detect it. The data give the number of cats which have a preference for this brand as a proportion of cats showing any preference.

3.   (a)   Suppose there is no difference in taste. If X is the number of times that the odd sample is correctly identified, then $X \sim B(8, \frac{1}{3})$.

$$P(X \geq 6) = \binom{8}{6}\left(\frac{1}{3}\right)^6\left(\frac{2}{3}\right)^2 + \binom{8}{7}\left(\frac{1}{3}\right)^7\left(\frac{2}{3}\right) + \binom{8}{8}\left(\frac{1}{3}\right)^8$$

$$\approx 0.020$$

The chance of 6 or more people choosing correctly at random is only 2%. This provides strong evidence that there are detectable differences.

(b)   No! It only tells you if the taster can tell the **difference** between the two types, not which is preferred.

4.   (a)   Each person would taste a reference sample such as a small piece of bread with butter. He or she would then be asked to taste samples of bread with butter and bread with margarine and match one of these with the reference sample. The samples would be allocated in a random order and must appear identical. (For example, they must have the same size and use the same bread, the same or similar quantity of butter or margarine, the same texture of butter or margarine and so on.)

(b)   Let X be the number of correct matches. Assuming that the tasters cannot actually detect a difference in taste, then $X \sim B(16, \frac{1}{2})$.

$$P(X \geq 12) = \binom{16}{12}\left(\frac{1}{2}\right)^{12}\left(\frac{1}{2}\right)^4 + \binom{16}{13}\left(\frac{1}{2}\right)^{13}\left(\frac{1}{2}\right)^3 + \dots + \binom{16}{16}\left(\frac{1}{2}\right)^{16}$$

$$\approx 0.0384$$

It is very unlikely that a result as extreme as 12 or more correct matches would have been obtained by guesswork alone. On this evidence, it is likely that people can distinguish between butter and margarine. Note again that no **preference** is expressed.

(continued)

5.   (a)   If there were no general preference for the new product, then as many would prefer it as would prefer the original. It is assumed that the tasters are equally likely to choose either the new or the original and so $P(N) = P(O) = \frac{1}{2}$.

Since 8 people were asked, the number who prefer the new variety has distribution $B(8, \frac{1}{2})$, assuming **independence**.

     (b)   5 out of 8 prefer the new variety.

$$P(X \geq 5) = \binom{8}{5}\left(\frac{1}{2}\right)^5\left(\frac{1}{2}\right)^3 + \binom{8}{6}\left(\frac{1}{2}\right)^6\left(\frac{1}{2}\right)^2 + \binom{8}{7}\left(\frac{1}{2}\right)^7\left(\frac{1}{2}\right)^1 + \binom{8}{8}\left(\frac{1}{2}\right)^8$$

$$\approx 0.363$$

The event of 5 or more people preferring the new variety could easily have occurred by chance.

4 Testing drugs

4.1 Clinical trials

> **(a)** Describe in outline how you would set up a clinical trial using patients already attending a clinic at Eastleigh Royal.
>
> **(b)** How would you try to ensure that any benefits or side-effects can be attributed to the use of B12546?
>
> **(c)** Describe some of the ethical problems which might affect the design of this clinical trial.

(a) A simple way of conducting the experiment would be to choose a sample of patients and administer the drug to all of them. Their blood pressures could be recorded at various times during the course of treatment. Other tests would also need to be carried out both to check for possible side-effects and to determine if there were other benefits, for example whether angina sufferers experience a reduction in the intensity and frequency of chest pains.

The results of the trial would be compared with records of patients receiving conventional treatments.

(b) A trial such as the one above is called an **uncontrolled trial**. It has been found that some patients improve because of the psychological effects of receiving a special treatment and so it is usual to have a **control group**. Patients in the control group would receive precisely the same treatment in terms of check-ups and additional medical attention, but would not take B12546. They would either be on a standard drug treatment or taking a **placebo**, something which looks like a drug but has no active ingredients.

Those supervising the trials can unwittingly introduce bias in various ways. Medically, it may seem appropriate to recommend patients for the trial on special grounds, for example, if they are not responding to conventional treatments. However, results from such trials might not be typical for all patients. Another way in which medical practitioners can unintentionally affect the results is through their attitude to patients using a treatment they especially believe in or about which they have strong reservations.

Statistically, the most satisfactory procedure is to have patients allocated at random to the treated group or the control group **and** for the medical staff not to know who has received which drug until after the trial. An experiment which has been set up in this way is called a **double blind test**. It can be arranged by having numbered boxes of drugs corresponding to some numbering of the patients.

Another possible problem concerns carry-over effects from previous treatments. In some cases it may be appropriate for patients to discontinue other drugs some time before participating in the experiment.

(c)   The use of human beings in trials raises a number of ethical questions. A doctor may understandably be concerned about using a new product which may have long-term side-effects if he or she is reasonably happy with a patient's prognosis using a standard treatment. Consequently, some new procedures are initially used on only the most seriously ill patients. When a new medical technique is only used on either the most dangerously ill patients or by the most skilled or experienced practitioners, then it is very difficult to obtain results of statistical significance from the initial findings.

A doctor may also be concerned about patients in the control group. If doctors believe a new treatment to be better, then they will be understandably reluctant to withhold this treatment from **any** of their patients. A balance must be achieved between the immediate needs of an individual patient and the long-term benefits of a genuine control group. In practice, it is unlikely that any patient would be given a placebo if there was even a very small chance of this leading to a deterioration in his or her condition, although a doctor might be happier to continue to prescribe a standard treatment.

One further ethical question concerns the extent to which patients should be told the truth about their treatment. One possibility is for the whole group to know that there will be a control group. Each individual could then agree to participate in the trial on the understanding that they will not be told which group they will be placed in.

This commentary may not have covered all of the issues raised by your own attempts to outline a possible clinical trial. It should, however, indicate that there are many difficulties connected with medical experiments. Statistical ideas play an increasingly important part in clinical decisions but, in any experiment, concern for individual patients will also affect experimental design.

Allocating treatments

1.   With this method of allocation it is likely that the two groups will not even be the same size. They are also unlikely to be similar with respect to age, weight or smoking habits. Such a method of allocation is therefore not suitable for dividing a small number of patients into a treatment group and a control group.

2.   The allocation can proceed as in question 1, stopping as soon as one of the groups has 8 patients. The following groups were obtained by one of the authors.

A	1, 2, 3, 8, 10, 11, 13, 14

Mean age 48.9 years (s.d. 10.2 years)
Mean weight 93.2 kg (s.d. 12.6 kg)
2 smokers, 6 non-smokers

B	4, 5, 6, 7, 9, 12, 15, 16

Mean age 45.6 years (s.d. 12.3 years)
Mean weight 77.2 kg (s.d. 6.2 kg)
5 smokers, 3 non-smokers

These two groups are only similar with respect to age. It is likely that the two groups you obtained are also not very similar.

3.   It can be very difficult to match patients on a number of variables. In this example, a reasonably good pairing can be obtained from a graph of weight against age.

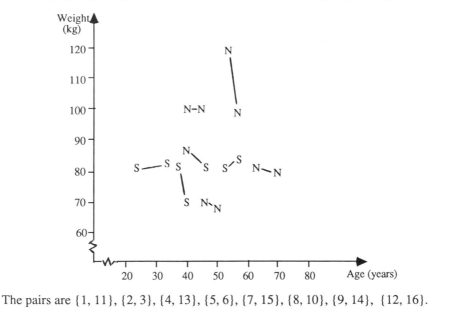

The pairs are {1, 11}, {2, 3}, {4, 13}, {5, 6}, {7, 15}, {8, 10}, {9, 14}, {12, 16}.

(continued)

71

4.   One of the authors obtained the following groups:

Pair	A	B
1	1	11
2	3	2
3	4	13
4	5	6
5	15	7
6	10	8
7	9	14
8	12	16

A   Mean age 45.9 years (s.d. 12.2 years)
        Mean weight 84.0 kg (s.d. 10.5 kg)
        3 smokers and 5 non-smokers

B   Mean age 48.6 years (s.d. 10.4 years)
        Mean weight 86.4 kg (s.d. 14.6 kg)
        4 smokers and 4 non-smokers

In view of the way the groups have been chosen, it is not surprising that they are very similar with respect to the baseline variables.

5.   Providing the most important factors have been considered in the baseline measurements, the matched-pair design offers better prospects of obtaining a control group which is genuinely similar to the treatment group.

Clinical trials often have to take place using relatively small groups of patients. In such cases, the parallel groups design can easily lead to groups which are very dissimilar. Any effects of the new drug can then be masked by the effects of the other variables such as age, weight and smoking habits.

Note

In practice, patients often come sequentially through the doors of a clinic. The most common method of forming the groups is then to use random allocation but with some form of stratification. The importance of randomness is that it increases the likelihood of matching with respect to **unknown** factors.

Analysis

1.   (a)   A patient who has just rushed to the clinic is likely to have a higher blood pressure than one who has been sitting and waiting. To remove any such bias, all the patients should lie down for an appropriate period of time before their blood pressures are measured.

    (b)   The three-week period was necessary so that the effects of any previous treatments would be eliminated by the time the new treatment was started.

2.

		Before	After
A	Mean	100.5	90.0
	Variance	171.0	68.8
B	Mean	96.9	96.9
	Variance	108.1	24.6

The average fall in blood pressure, 10.5 mm for A and 0 for B, gives a simple comparison between the two groups. Generally, the results of an experiment will be measured in terms of a **change** in a variable.

3.   It is, perhaps, better to draw separate tables for each group. Listing results systematically makes it easier to see patterns and, in the tables below, the patients have been arranged in order of decreasing blood pressure at the start of the treatment. Alternatively, they could have been arranged according to some other known variable, for example by weight or age.

Since it is the change in blood pressure which is of interest, it is useful to have this in a separate column in the table.

Group A

Patient	Blood pressure (mm)		
	3 weeks	4 weeks	change
1	120	100	− 20
4	106	90	− 16
3	105	90	− 15
11	103	95	− 8
13	100	75	− 25
9	100	90	− 10
15	100	100	0
6	70	80	+ 10

Group B

Patient	Blood pressure (mm)		
	3 weeks	4 weeks	change
7	110	100	− 10
2	110	105	− 5
14	105	95	− 10
8	100	100	0
16	95	100	+ 5
12	88	95	+ 7
5	85	90	+ 5
10	82	90	+ 8

(continued)

4.   A reduction in blood pressure has been measured in almost all patients receiving B12546. This can be seen clearly in the table for group A which is given in the answer to question 3.

The results from the control group do not show such a trend and so are useful in indicating that the reductions are due to B12546 and not to some other aspect of the experiments which was common to both group A and group B.

Since this was a parallel groups trial, chance variations between the two groups in the baseline variables would need to be considered. Furthermore, a statistical test would need to be employed to check how likely it is for results such as these to occur simply by chance. However, it does appear that B12546 has reduced blood pressure for male patients with original blood pressures of between 105 and 115 mm.

1.   (a)   The volunteers could be numbered 1 to 100 in order of registering. Using a table of random digits and reading them off in pairs, the first 50 distinct passengers can be identified. (You will need to use 00 to mean 100.) The first 25 volunteers identified can be given C184 and the remaining 25 can be given *Staywell*.

        (b)   The fact that C184 and *Staywell* are being given on the **same trip** ensures that both treatments are being tested under the same conditions, such as the time of day and the weather.

        (c)   Psychological factors are known to be significant for all forms of travel sickness. It is therefore especially important that the volunteers should not know which treatment they are receiving. Knowing which drug a patient had taken could also affect the way an observer might interpret and record any results.

        (d)   The sample size is quite small and so, by chance, the treatment and control groups may be quite dissimilar in terms of how acutely they suffer from sea-sickness.

2.   (a)   Perhaps the most important question is how acutely each passenger suffers from sea-sickness. You are also likely to have considered asking for age, gender and weight. You may have thought of many other factors but the questionnaire should be as short as possible.

        (b)   One volunteer would be selected at random from each matched pair. These could be allocated C184 and the remaining volunteers would receive *Staywell*.

        (c)   The effect of some of the variable factors which might affect the results would be eliminated by this experimental design. It is particularly important that volunteers should be matched according to their susceptibility to sea-sickness.

3.   The wash-out period is the period between the two journeys. This will vary from person to person. The prevailing sea conditions during a crossing will to some extent determine whether or not a volunteer has sea-sickness. Everyone has the same conditions on the outward journey but some volunteers are taking C184 and some *Staywell* during that voyage. The volunteers are all returning on different crossings with different sea conditions and so the results of this experiment could be seriously misleading.

DATASHEETS

Forestry data

Region 1

Area	Small	Large	Total	Area	Small	Large	Total	Area	Small	Large	Total
1	97	142	239	25	75	128	203	49	92	136	228
2	77	113	190	26	87	117	204	50	86	123	209
3	75	126	201	27	71	121	192	51	91	135	226
4	91	165	256	28	107	142	249	52	92	125	217
5	92	136	228	29	90	148	238	53	92	131	223
6	77	106	183	30	78	113	191	54	89	121	210
7	106	143	249	31	88	131	219	55	91	123	214
8	83	143	226	32	107	147	254	56	89	144	233
9	86	135	221	33	83	126	209	57	94	136	230
10	99	142	241	34	79	111	190	58	77	132	209
11	69	107	176	35	77	125	202	59	84	125	209
12	92	149	241	36	95	145	240	60	85	136	221
13	88	133	221	37	77	112	189	61	82	121	203
14	92	132	224	38	74	114	188	62	90	138	228
15	74	127	201	39	93	153	246	63	86	128	214
16	78	135	213	40	85	137	222	64	77	116	193
17	92	135	227	41	95	144	239	65	88	111	199
18	75	120	195	42	94	142	236	66	110	146	256
19	97	137	234	43	79	131	210	67	88	146	234
20	84	126	210	44	80	118	198	68	84	143	227
21	87	128	215	45	84	114	198	69	91	139	230
22	87	138	225	46	80	127	207	70	81	124	205
23	87	134	221	47	105	158	263	71	79	123	202
24	87	134	221	48	76	122	198	72	93	149	242

(continued)

Region 2

Area	Small	Large	Total	Area	Small	Large	Total	Area	Small	Large	Total
73	114	232	346	105	97	208	305	137	105	186	291
74	91	189	280	106	93	186	279	138	130	240	370
75	86	209	295	107	89	207	296	139	100	240	340
76	101	268	369	108	110	238	348	140	96	234	330
77	108	224	332	109	91	186	277	141	105	228	333
78	92	177	269	110	86	190	276	142	94	206	300
79	125	234	359	111	107	249	356	143	92	203	295
80	95	233	328	112	98	225	323	144	107	243	350
81	100	222	322	113	110	236	346	145	106	217	323
82	116	233	349	114	109	232	341	146	104	224	328
83	81	179	260	115	91	215	306	147	111	256	367
84	106	242	348	116	94	196	290	148	100	232	332
85	102	220	322	117	101	189	290	149	136	270	406
86	108	218	326	118	92	210	302	150	77	162	239
87	85	209	294	119	121	258	379	151	126	239	365
88	90	221	311	120	88	202	290	152	102	239	341
89	107	222	329	121	107	224	331	153	112	255	367
90	87	199	286	122	101	204	305	154	100	211	311
91	113	226	339	123	106	222	328	155	93	196	289
92	99	208	307	124	110	207	317	156	121	239	360
93	102	211	313	125	109	216	325	157	107	253	360
94	101	226	327	126	106	200	306	158	100	226	326
95	101	221	322	127	107	205	312	159	104	218	322
96	102	220	322	128	102	236	338	160	98	241	339
97	86	211	297	129	110	224	334	161	90	201	291
98	103	195	298	130	88	217	305	162	86	207	293
99	83	199	282	131	99	207	306	163	94	196	290
100	126	234	360	132	98	224	322	164	88	201	289
101	103	242	345	133	97	199	296	165	118	256	374
102	92	189	281	134	105	226	331	166	104	189	293
103	104	215	319	135	101	211	312	167	107	238	345
104	125	241	366	136	90	193	283	168	103	241	344